# #PuttingMy F*cking Self First

## A HASHTAG BOOK BY SKELL

EDITED BY **DR. ALLISON MATHEWS**
PICTURES BY **JESSICA E. BOYD**

**SIT WITH SKELL**

Copyright © 2020 by Jeskell Creecy

All Rights Reserved.
Published in the United States by Sit With Skell
sitwithskell.com

ISBN 978-0-578-77825-9

Printed in the United States of America

# FOREWARD

By Dr. Allison Mathews

Wow. I am so proud of my line sister, Jeskell. This book is raw and personal, funny and timely. This book shows her commitment to continuing to push herself to grow and share her words of wisdom from tough lessons throughout her life. I feel honored to have been asked to edit, *#PuttingMyF*ckingSelfFirst*, not only because Jeskell is my dear friend and line sister, but because it also forced me to face my past and heal. Jeskell uses humor and colloquialisms in a modern and innovative way to create a first of its kind hashtag book. I believe her stories transcend generations and will resonate with old and young audiences alike. As you read through each chapter, I urge you to feel every emotion. Laugh. Cry. Nod your head in agreement. Shake your head in judgement. Reflect. And then share your own stories and revelations on social media or over a glass of wine with your girlfriends!

I hope you enjoy reading this book as much as I enjoyed editing it.

# WHO DOESN'T LOVE A GOOD HASHTAG?

Hashtags are catchy. They're simple. They can be long or short. We use them to bring about social change or to promote a new product. You literally have to be a sociopath not to love hashtags.

This hashtag book is a long time coming for me. When I was in the second grade, I used to take computer paper, staple it together, and write children's books. I always knew I wanted to be an author. To come full circle and write this book is therapeutic for me. I wanted to share this therapy with you.

You will find my heart on these pages. You will find my embarrassment. You will find my joy. I own it all because it
has made me into the woman I am today. Everything I have been through was worth it. I can honestly say that at this point in my life… again, a long time coming. I hope you can see yourself in these stories. I hope you can begin or appreciate your healing journey. I hope you can learn from my mistakes. I hope you laugh. I hope you cry. I hope you say, "Me too, sis!"

Each lesson starts with a hashtag based on my personal experience. I wanted the hashtags to be relatable. I really want you to get to know me through these pages. I haven't always been an open and vulnerable person. So, to share these stories with you is the result of a lot of inner work. I'm so glad that I HAVE ARRIVED… again, a long time coming!

## CHAPTER 1
# #PuttingMyF*ckingSelfFirst

Putting my FUCKING self first. Straight like that! No chaser.

I know, a pretty intense way to start a book. GOOD! I hope it grabbed your attention because one day you will be sick and tired of putting others before yourself.

One day you will be sick and tired of overextending yourself.

One day you'll be tired of *"burning both ends of the candle,"* as my stepmom would say.

DO NOT be like me. I waited until I hit rock bottom. I waited until I had no choice but to deal with myself because there was no one else around to deal with. The year I had to finally face myself was one of the hardest in my life. It's still an ongoing process, but now I have the tools to handle things much differently than I did a year ago.

I felt I needed to control people. If I put on my mask and pretended to be someone I was not, people wouldn't leave me.

This all stemmed from abandonment issues I developed after my mom died (that story is a hashtag for a different page). If I was a perfect child, my family would love me the most. If I overextended myself or my resources, my friend would tell everyone I was the best.

If I compromised myself for a romantic interest, he wouldn't leave me. Nobody could ever measure up to those expectations because the real problem was not the people around me. So, I went to therapy. Through therapy I realized you must deal with your shit, or you'll be doomed to relive the same experiences until you do. The only person I have control over is me. Honestly, that was a relief. I realized I had to put me first and heal to be able to show up for the people that mattered. Then I had to figure out the people who mattered.

The healing process is sometimes more painful than the trauma. I spent years only allowing myself to experience anger to suppress the fear, guilt, and sadness I was experiencing. Like a famous Instagram meme once said, "Anger is a sadness protector." WOAH. I feel seen. When I started healing, I allowed myself to experience every emotion. And it hurt like hell because I wasn't used to feeling sadness well up in my eyes, or vulnerability form a knot in my chest. Now I have a much better grasp on how my body reacts to emotions and what those emotions are trying to tell me. Believe me, you can, too. I am a living testimony.

# CHAPTER 2
# #StopTheSearchSis

Don't play. You know what the search is. You think you need proof of what your dude is up to, so you go snooping through his phone. You check the girl's social media. You look through his personal belongings. In reality, you didn't need to do any of that. *Your intuition tells you everything you need to know.*

I'm going to be vulnerable right now and tell you my truth. My ex-boyfriend and I were talking about exchanging keys. I just knew our relationship was progressing. Then one day he came to me and said, "we needed a break" but he "didn't want us to talk to other people."

Pause.

What?!

Resume.

Right then, my intuition went off like a superhero in a comic book.

I was heartbroken, but instead of telling him how I really felt, I played the tough role and decided to go along with it. My intuition told me that he was dealing with his ex-girlfriend. I kept brushing the notion off. His social media did not give any hints, and she was private (punk ass).

One day, I had to go to work super early in the morning. I decided to ride by his house. As soon as I turned the corner, I saw his ex-girlfriend's car in his driveway. I pulled up and hopped out the car. I knew then why we needed a break, and I didn't get a key. I contemplated banging on his door. I ended up sending him a picture message of her car and a well thought out break-up message... that I regret to this day! I should have broken down that door and whooped his ass.

Pause.

I don't condone violence.

Or making a fool of yourself in front of another woman. I'm just keeping it real about how I felt at the time.

Resume.

What I really should have done was trusted my instinct during the initial conversation and called him out on his bull. I had to learn how my body reacted when my instinct was triggered so that I could recognize when to react more quickly. Most importantly, I had to learn that I'm not going to steer myself wrong. I had to learn how to treat myself so that I could teach others through my actions.

**NO ONE SAID BEING A GROWN ASS WOMAN WAS EASY.**

GABRIELLE UNION

## CHAPTER 3
# #DancingWithDepression

I have suffered from anxiety and depression for most of my twenties and now into my thirties. Now, I'm not talking about the type of depression you see in the movies—a person laying in bed crying with the covers over their head. My depression was and is more subtle. I am a very high-functioning person who is depressed. I have always been involved in many extracurricular activities; I have lots of friends. I have a very supportive family. None of that mattered in the beginning, because I felt like happiness came from an outside source. If I got one more good grade, raise at work, a boyfriend… then I would finally become happy.

When I used to tell my friends that I was depressed, they would try to convince me that I wasn't. I know they meant well. They would remind me of all things that I had, all the friends around me, and how pretty I looked. And because I never wanted to be depressed in the first place, I tried to buy into their compliments, but it never lasted long. I viewed the world as cloudy. I figured that my life was supposed to be bad days with occasional good moments. I experienced a terrible breakup before my thirty-first birthday. The kind that makes you curl into a ball on the floor and wonder how you ever let your heart be that open. I happened to have a doctor's appointment in the middle of it and my doctor was the person who saw the signs before I did.

My doctor isn't a Black woman, but she's a woman of color. I told her that I wanted a person of color that will listen to me and not fall into the stereotyping of Black woman. I love her. During my visit, she asked basic questions, and I gave basic answers. Then she stopped and said, "I think you should take anxiety and depression medication." I looked at her like she was crazy. I told her I was ok, and I would just keep seeing my therapist. Once I got home, I figured, how could life get any worse. I researched natural medication and came across the pills I currently take—I call them my Superwoman Pills. The world is no longer cloudy. My life is still far from perfect, but I now understand it doesn't have to be. I no longer need a person, an object, or an event to bring me temporary joy. Happiness is nowhere I'm not, everywhere I go, and wherever I am.

A dance is close and intimate; there's no way to ignore your dance partner. I'm going to confront depression and not just hope it just goes away. I'm a pretty good dancer. I'm not going to hide any part of this dance with depression so you can see how it's done.

## CHAPTER 4
## #MoMoneyMoMoves

BUDGET. I know. When I used to hear the "B" word, I said the exact same thing. *"It's my money after I pay my bills. Whatever is left over is for me." "I work hard every day. I deserve this!"* But hear me out. When I earned a paycheck that had a comma in my first job, you couldn't tell me nothin'! After the essentials, I brought high-end clothing and took lavish trips... and I was living paycheck to paycheck. So, I decided to work more hours. But I was still living paycheck to paycheck. When that didn't work, I took another job with a higher salary. Yet I was still living paycheck to paycheck, and I couldn't understand why.

Nobody ever talked to me about money growing up. The only money advice my mom ever gave me was, "Don't get a bunch of credit cards." She never even told me WHY. I never took a finance or tax course in school. (BUT ask me to explain the Pythagorean theorem and I'm your girl). I did not know the difference between assets and liabilities. I didn't know what a 401k was or WHY you would need it. And when it came to borrowing money, my thought process was, "I mean they wouldn't offer it if they didn't think you could pay it back right? The only reason I saved was because I didn't make enough to buy what I wanted as a kid… but now I'm making commas baby! Who needs to save?!"

I had debt from so many different sources. Two credit cards, a store card, a hospital bill, two personal loans, a car, and student loans. Crazy thing is, I worked so much I could have paid things off quickly. Most of the time, I didn't even need to use a credit card. I just did not know where my money was going. I swiped and swiped and swiped and looked up and had more days left until the next paycheck than I had money.

One day my coworker asked me, "How are you doing with saving your money?" and it led me to stop and think about my spending habits. The rest was history.

I had to rethink my approach to money. A budget is not restrictive; it is security. I tell my money where to go. (And I love being in charge.) With a budget, I do not worry if I'm taking money out of one need to pay another. With a budget, I was able to pay off over $20k in debt. With a budget, I felt like I made Mo' Money because I was able to see where I was spending frivolously. Nowadays, I can save up for trips and the high-end items I want. Do not get it twisted: I still work side jobs to continue to meet my financial objectives. I've worked overtime. I've trained people in the gym, and I've delivered food. I read finance books and listened to podcasts to help me understand how finances work. They also taught me how to understand human behavior and how it relates to money and finances. My ultimate goal is to be debt-free and leave a legacy for my future children.

Mo' money only leads to more issues if you care more about looking rich than being wealthy. With Mo' Money I make Mo' Moves based on what I want to do and not what I need to do to make ends meet.

> **THINK LIKE A QUEEN. A QUEEN IS NOT AFRAID TO FAIL. FAILURE IS ANOTHER STEPPING STONE TO GREATNESS.**
>
> — OPRAH WINFREY

CHAPTER 5

# #FriendshipLuvLanguage

I'm not sure why that as women, we are not taught to cultivate our friendships. There are tons of magazine articles, books, IG Lives, etc. that teach us how to improve our romantic relationships: communicate better, listen more, use "I" statements. We never mention, however, that all of those principals can be used to enhance our platonic relationships, too... especially with our girlfriends! Just like with your romantic partner, you can heal, grow, and evolve. We need to pay way more attention to each other.

I lost a friend, and now I understand. Reflecting on our friendship, I recognize that she may have felt like she was a better friend to me than I was to her. I had a terrible job that I didn't make a lot of money doing. She was the type of friend who usually fronted the bill. She was usually the first to text and the one that visited the most. I would go to her job, drink all the caramel macchiatos I wanted, and never paid for a thing. I had this huge twenty-fifth birthday blowout. She was there for all the planning, stress, headaches, and she helped me pay for some of it. Of course, I invited a lot of people to attend. I think she was jealous because I was showing attention to all my other friends. I think she wanted me to make her spot known to everyone else. We spoke briefly about the party. I tried to explain to her that I was just being a good hostess. That was the last day we spoke.

I'll take the majority of the blame for how our relationship ended. I want to say I was still a good friend to her, maybe just not in the ways she wanted. I could have figured out her "friendship luv language." We both could have done a better job of communicating to each other. I think we both just figured the other one, "should know how I feel." I could have told her I didn't make a lot of money and how much she meant to me (because I really did value our friendship). She could have told me if she was feeling used or anything else that was bottled up inside. I really think her reaction to the party was really a result of all her built-up emotions.

Fast Forward.

I sent her a message on social media telling her, "Happy 31st Birthday." She never replied. Oh, you were expecting a happy ending? Me, too. But life doesn't always happen like that. Maybe one day she will though. Since then, I am more conscious about calling and video chatting my friends just to say hey or tell them I love them. Before I unload a heavy emotional story on them, I try to ask if they're in a good headspace to listen. When they unload a heavy story on me, I try not to take the attention by talking about a relatable story I may have experienced. I let my friends know when they've hurt my feelings or when I need attention from them. I love girl's nights and girl's trips. I try to support all my friends' projects WITHOUT asking for a discount. I value my friendships so much more partly because I know how it feels to lose a good friend.

**OKAY, LADIES, NOW LET'S GET IN FORMATION.**

BEYONCÉ

# CHAPTER 6
# #StrengthInStandingStill

My mom passed two days before my eighteenth birthday and two days after her forty second birthday. The doctor gave her a certain amount of time to live. I don't know how long it was. I do know that she lived longer than what they told her. My parents didn't tell my brother and me. The whole time, they just told us mom was sick and the doctors are trying to figure out what's wrong. She told us the day after her birthday that she was dying. I now believe that she knew it was time. I can't imagine what was going through her mind, or how scared she was, or how at peace she was with it all. I go back and forth all the time trying to decide if it was right of them not to tell us. I was a typical teenager at the time. I cared more about being around my friends than my family. I spent my whole senior year trying to be around my friends when I could have spent the time around her. I know that's normal for a regular senior, but not at the expense of not spending the last days of my mother's life with her. I'm sure she wanted to keep life as normal as possible for her and us. I'm sure she didn't want us to be worried or scared. I'm sure if they did tell us, I'd be arguing a different point in this story right now. I realized that her decision just is what it is. It is was hers. It was neither wrong nor right, but something she had to do for her.

Death is... final. And I know you looked at the statement and said 'duh.' But you don't know what that means until the memories of your dad and brother evolve, but your mom is stuck in time. Or when you look up in the stands at graduation and your mom isn't there. Or when you move into your first grownup apartment and she's not bringing in boxes behind you. Or when your nephew calls someone Nana that's not your mama. And you feel bad about saying that statement out loud because you love your stepmom and you love your mom. And you love the life you live now with the people in it, and you miss what life would have been like. Your dad's hair is doing that cute salt and pepper thing and your brother is over six feet tall with a family of his own. And your mama is still forty-two with red lipstick and red nails. And when you dream about her and ask where she is, she just stares at you and says nothing. And because of all this you develop abandonment issues.

When she died, I felt I had to be strong for everyone else. Yeah, I know it sounds crazy to me, too! MY mom died, and I had to be strong for everyone else. The crazy thing is nobody told me I had to do any of this. I made this task up in my head to avoid feeling the real emotions. I didn't trust that I would be able to pick myself up if I went down that rabbit hole. I wish I would have grown up in a way that I was able to talk to people about my problems. That avoidance turned into abandonment issues. I blamed my mom for leaving me, and I figured everyone else in my life would follow suit. I kept that avoidance/abandonment cycle throughout my twenties. I avoided tough conversations and tough feelings and as soon as I got close to someone, I would find a reason to leave, so they wouldn't leave me first. Whew! My therapist had a lot to unpack.

I didn't realize any of this at first. I just made up new things to busy myself with… all to avoid myself. My therapist taught me there was strength in standing still. I had to get over the guilt of not grieving my mom "properly." As I get older, I think about small ways I can still honor my mom, like the picture I have of her in my favorite frame. I hate that my mom will never get to meet my (very) future husband and (very) future kids, but I will keep her memory alive by telling them all about her. I want to play her favorite song at my (very) future wedding.

I had to realize when I was letting my abandonment anxiety cloud my judgement. There's always the possibility that a person can leave. Then I think, the person closest to me left and I survived. Not only did I survive…. I THRIVED and currently I'm THRIVING. I know my mother would be proud of me. So, if I can make it through her death, would it really be that bad if someone walked out of my life? If I put my all into a worthy person, and we didn't work out, then at least I will never have to wonder, "What if?" Also, I can leave! If someone isn't a good fit —family, friends, or lover—I shouldn't stay just because of the time we spent together or whatever reasons we convince ourselves to stay in toxic relationships. I want to stay with someone because we fit, because we support each other, because we make each other laugh, because we can sit around and do nothing and still have a good time, and because we love each other enough to call us out on our bullshit. And I want that for you, too.

# THE PEOPLE YOU LOVE NEVER DIE.

**UNKNOWN**

# CHAPTER 7
# #DoingLifeMyWay

Like most young, ambitious, go-getters my age, I had my life totally planned out by eighteen. I was going to college and would meet my husband, graduate in four years, get married, buy a house, then have two kids before 30.

Fast forward. I'm thirty-one with no kids, living in an apartment that I love with my roommate. I guess someone swept my feet with a broom when I was younger.

Speaking of myths, let's get into all the things I was told to do to achieve the 'dream'. My mom used to stress the importance of going to school and pursuing a career. My aunties used to point to my cousins and say, "Don't be like such and such and have all them babies." My dad said, "Make sure you go to an HBCU so you can meet your husband in college." I worked my ass off in school. When I got my first 'C' I cried.

I was president of this club and played basketball for that team. I went to college and focused on having a career so I could be a desirable partner. I worked out in the gym so I could have the perfect body. (Don't get it twisted, I do look good naked.) I thought I had the correct formula, until all my friends started getting engaged. I had friends get engaged that didn't have as many degrees as I did, weren't as active in school, had kids before marriage, and didn't work out nearly as much as I did. All that pressure, for what?

Now that I'm over thirty, I get asked all the time, "When am I going to get married or have children?" I get told I don't have that much time left.

So, wait a minute – When I was younger, it was, "Don't have kids yet!" Now that I'm older, it is, "What are you waiting for?" Make it make sense! I was so focused on all these 'suggestions' on how to live my life that I did it their way, and they still weren't satisfied.

I had to decide to live my life my way. I started prioritizing my dreams. I started taking trips out of the country with my friends. Now, I'm living with a roommate so I can save money and buy my own house.

Sure, my biggest dream is still to become a mom and an amazing partner. But why should I have to wait on a man or anybody besides myself to make my dream come true? I have looked into alternative options to have children. I'm picking and choosing which societal norms and non-traditional methods of doing life best serve me.

Will you join me?

# I'M SICK OF MOTHAFUCKAS TRY'NA TELL ME HOW TO LIVE.

**MEG THEE STALLION**

## CHAPTER 8
## #AintNoMicDropBih

I do not know why adults do not see children as people. I was the type of kid who you could not say, "Because I said so!" to and let it fly. Even as a child, that made no sense. My whole life, I felt like I had to prove to people that my opinion was worthy. My dad has changed over the years. He has let go of a lot of the societal norms of masculinity. When I was a child, that was different. I felt like he wanted to stifle my voice. Those early childhood experiences spilled over into my adult life. I dated men who I had to constantly battle to prove my opinion and worth—like with my father.

Then, I became the only Black person in White spaces. I was one of two Black people in my program in school. So of course, I had the weight of the whole race on my shoulders. One day, my classmate asked me what "truffle butter" was. I literally told them I was not the expert on all things Black and pointed to my White classmate (who bragged about dating Black men) and told them to ask her.

At work, people also have tried to discredit me. Because I'm a woman, or Black, or petite. One day, I was trying to encourage my patient to participate in his physical therapy session. He was being an asshole about it. He asked if I was married, insinuating that because I was so stern that I wasn't feminine enough to be married. I asked him if he was married and he said he had been married twice. I said, "I can tell." As a Black woman, I constantly have to assert myself as valuable and respected to both White folks and Black men.

To protect myself, I have learned to be very vocal on my needs. I have probably expressed, "What you said has hurt my feelings," more times in the last year than I have said in my entire life. I have been vocal about racial injustices. I have been vocal about women's rights. I do not want anyone to ever have to wonder what my stance is on life. I no longer have time to convince people that my opinion is worthy. I realized that it's not me. People lack vision into their own worth. If they can't see themselves, how can I expect them to see me?

Today, my dad is proud of how I stand up for myself, for what's right, and for people who cannot stand up for themselves. He tells me that he thinks I'm going to be the mayor one day. He tells me how smart I am. It means the world to me. This also shows me you can't worry about what other people have to say. If you believe enough in a cause, and especially in yourself, you have to speak on it. Even if no one else has your back. Ain't no mic drop. The world is going to hear every word I have to say.

**SUCCESS IS LIKING YOURSELF, LIKING WHAT YOU DO, AND LIKING HOW YOU DO IT.**

**MAYA ANGELOU**

**CHAPTER 9**
# #ThankYouForBeingBlack

**MY ODE TO BLACK PEOPLE:**

I love Black People's **laugh**. It comes from the most genuine place in the world. Because we know pain and sorrow.

I love Black People's **golden skin color**. As it ages, it becomes more vibrant. Black People rarely look their age.

I love Black People's **fight**. From birth, there are obstacles put in place to keep us discouraged and beaten. But we keep elevating and progressing.

I love Black People's **style**. Black people know how to make nothing look like something! Black people envision a design and bring it to life. Black people tell the rest of the world what is in, and what is out.

I love Black People's **hair**. It's delicate. It has to be wrapped in silk and oils. We have to protect it and allow it to grow. Then we bring it out on special occasions like fine china.

I love Black People's **heart**. It's a heart so pure. Black people have so much compassion. Black people have so much love to freely give. Black people take care of each other. Black people look out for each other. Black people do not give up hope.

I want Black people to **rest**. We have worked ourselves to disease and death for centuries.

I want us to **live** and **enjoy life**.

I want us to die **without regretting** the time we didn't spend taking care of ourselves.

I want Black People to **heal** from generational trauma. We can no longer survive if we continue to live by "what goes on in this house, stays in this house" or "because I said so."

I want Black People to be **free**. Free from debt and stress so we can enjoy the world around us.

I want Black women to **forget about respectability politics**. It doesn't work for us. We can be whatever the hell we want to be. The rest do NOT get to decide… and we aren't the rest of the world's saviors either.

I want us to continue to **uplift** one another, support Black businesses, and support Black schools.

## CHAPTER 10
# #ChooseYourself

At the beginning of every year, I pick a word that will define my year. I write the word in huge letters and hang it in a place I look at every day. The word somehow seeps into your subconscious, and you start to believe you are the word and believe you can embody the word.

My word for the year is **FEARLESS.**

This year I took it a step further and made a mission statement for my year:

**I will not let fear stop me from trying new things, following my heart, manifesting my destiny, or loving myself unconditionally.**

Your hopes, your dreams, your desires. The fear of failing is not worth YOU. The fear of rejection is not worth YOU. Choose yourself every time, and I promise you'll never lose. So many times, I let fear stop me from pursing my dreams. So many great ideas lost to time. I missed out on opportunity after opportunity. Like studying abroad or starting a job in a new state. I used a lot negative self-talk. I told myself that I was undesirable and a burden to others. Oh! And don't let me make a mistake. Then I was stupid and unworthy. Oftentimes, I would say to myself "who wants to hear what you have to say or do?"

Now I tell myself if no one cares about what I have to say… FUCK THEM. I care what I have to say! My words hold value, and I deserve to take up space in this world. And I mean really, there are billions of people on this earth. I'm sure at least one person will find my life experiences useful.

In such uncertain times, when you literally don't know what the next day will bring, what do you have to lose? In times that are not so uncertain, what do you have to lose?

Yourself, if you're not careful.

I've lost myself a few times throughout life. After I didn't get into graduate school, I felt like a complete failure. After I pulled up and seen ol' girl car at my boyfriend's house, I felt like God was saying, marriage and kids weren't for me. After realizing I was twenty-eight with no romantic prospects, no house, no children, no graduate degree, and no money in the bank, I knew that I had to make a change. I knew that I had to find myself for the first time. I had to decide what Skell wanted. Not what everyone else wanted. I had to choose myself.

This journey to finding Skell has been everything but easy. Sometimes I ached so bad inside I would have done anything… to feel nothing again. Other times I felt like I had life all figured out. Nowadays, I have this overwhelmingly calm feeling that everything is going to be alright. Whether things turn out as I planned or take a sharp turn, everything comes full circle. Everything ends with me learning a valuable life lesson. I know how to handle wins and I know how to handle losses. I wake up every day and ask God to order my steps. Nobody has to deal with the consequences but me. Exactly how I like it.

I believe that we go through tough experiences to help the next person make it through theirs. We experience trauma, trials, and triumph to help or inspire others. And as the cliche goes, "If I help at least one person, I've done my job." I hope you are that person.

**DEDICATION**

This book is dedicated to my mom. The person who I watched take care of two children, a house, and a husband while dying of cancer. She was at every football game, every step team competition, every prom dress shopping appointment. Ma didn't miss a beat, and she never complained. She never made excuses. She's my muse.

I also dedicate this book to 2nd grade Jeskell, who was clearly far ahead of her time. She had enough insight to know our future. She was a badass who followed her gut. Maybe I should have listened to her a long time ago.

To my editor, my mentor, my cheerleader, my friend, my line sister Dr. Allison Mathews. Thank you for being there for me with ALL the things you have going on. You are such a role model and inspiration to me. My favorite line is, "I will school you, sis."

Thank you to my daddy. My first love. My first superhero. Thank you for always pushing me to be better. Thank you for your big hugs, forehead kisses, and daddy-daughter dates. Thank you for calling me "sweetie" and "baby girl". Thank you for being the ultimate girl dad and never allowing me to settle or make excuses.

Thanks to my stepmother, Robin. Thank you for being my friend who I do hoodrat things with. Thank you for calling me your bonus daughter during a time where I needed a woman's love.

To the second oldest, Brent, the gentle giant. Thank you for always being the first person to support and let people know about all my book reviews.

To my beautiful sister, Whitney. I love how our relationship has grown within the past two years. I love how both our big personalities allow the other to take up space.

To my rock and baby brother, Tony. Thank you for always holding me to a standard by being the first person who looks up to me. Thank you for being my best friend. Thank you for being my confidant. My roll dog and my ride or die.

Jasmine. The little sister I never knew I needed. I watched you grow into a woman right in front of my eyes. We have fussed, we have fought, and we have cried on each other's shoulders. I wouldn't change our relationship for the world.

Tasha, thank you for being like a mother to me. Thank you for never judging me and for helping me to grow as a woman. Thank you for making space for me, even though you have a biological daughter.

To my uncle, aunts, and cousins. I love how close our family is. I love how we always uplift and encourage one another. I love Thanksgiving, Christmases, and Birthdays… and it's because I know we will all get together and love on one another.

Thank you to my nephews, Tristan and Reece, for being my little dads. Always in my business and holding me accountable.

Thank you Alexxis, Nick, Gill, Brittany, Six, Patrice, Dunny, DJ, and all my friends that have been so supportive through all my endeavors. The countless texts and voice messages. The encouragement. The support. The love… even the tough love… Thank you, thank you, thank you! I did it, ya'll! I wrote a book!

Sit with Skell is a modern book club that brings POC to books by authors of color. Through videos and book discussions, Sit with Skell fosters a conversation centered around reading and reflection. Subscribe to Sit with Skell on YouTube and follow on Instagram.

www.ingramcontent.com/pod-product-compliance
Lightning Source LLC
Chambersburg PA
CBHW041401160426
42811CB00101B/1508